amuse-bouche

(Ah-MOOZE boosh) French, noun

1 A small complimentary appetizer offered by the chef just before dinner.

2 The literal translation (from French): amuse (amuse) + bouche (mouth) = "amuse-mouth" or "mouth-amuser"

3 A tiny bite that gives an idea of the chef's approach to food.

4 An appetizing little poem about food to be read aloud just before dinner or any time at all.

(See also A MOOSE BOOSH.)

*To my big brother who
inspired me to be a poet.
To my loving wife who
listens to my every poem.*

—Shabazz

Readers *to* Eaters

READERS to EATERS Books
12437 SE 26th Place, Bellevue, WA 98005
ReadersToEaters.com
Distributed by Publishers Group West

MIX
Paper from
responsible sources
FSC www.fsc.org **FSC® C002589**

Book design by Red Herring Design
Book production by The Kids at Our House

The artwork started with photographs taken by Larkin, who then
added a layer of doodles with white paint, digitally rendered.

All my friends, family, neighbors and coworkers who appear in these photos are the champions of this book.
Every picture was taken on the streets of New York City where I play, in the homes of my faith community
where I pray, or in Virginia where my family lives and feeds me. Thank you. Special thanks to Ashley Larkin,
my wife, who helped me produce every photo in this book. —E.-S. L.

The text is set in Avenir, designed in 1988 by Adrian Frutiger. The word *avenir* means "future" in French.
While Frutiger based his design on historical geometric sans-serif fonts like Futura, he introduced
nuances that make Avenir more organic, legible, and suited to modern typographic needs.

10 9 8 7 6 5 4 3 2 1
First Edition
Library of Congress Control Number: 2014944375
ISBN: 978-0-9836615-5-9

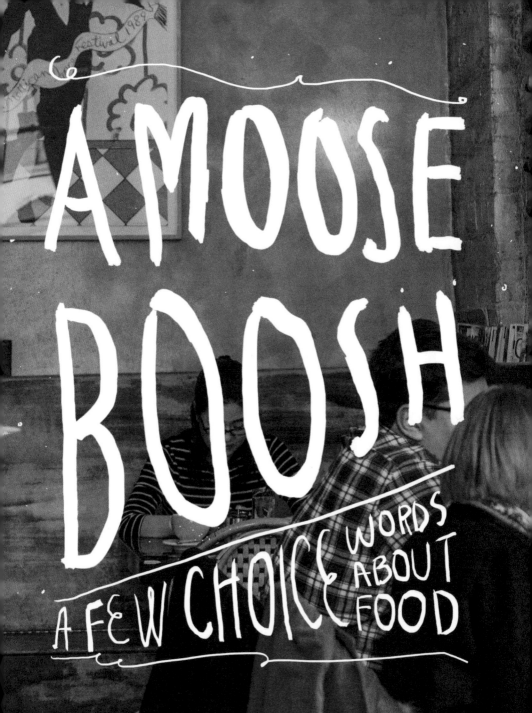

A MOOSE BOOSH

A FEW CHOICE WORDS ABOUT FOOD

ERIC-SHABAZZ LARKIN

MENU

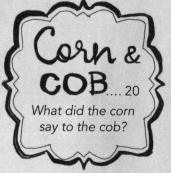
Red
ROOSTER,
RED
Rooster
..... 42

 A MOOSE BOOSH

So I said, "Sorry, sir, I did not order this...
  this most peculiar dish."

"No," the waiter said. "It's an *amuse-bouche*,
  compliments of the chef."

"Ah, well, that's very nice. So what's the compliment?"

"No, there is no compliment, just this tiny little dish."

"But I told you already that I did not order this."

"No, what I'm trying to say is that this is the chef's gift."

"Oh, I understand. My apology.
  I just have one more question.
  I don't mean to push,
  but did you call this a Moose Boosh?"

"No, sir, it's a French word, a bit abstruse.
  It's an amuse-bouche. And tasty, too."

MY FATHER IS A PAINTER

My father is a painter,
but he doesn't use a brush.
My plate is his canvas,
the colors are so lush.

Purple cabbage and red kimchi,
yellow curry and green kale.
The tastes are the brushstrokes
that tell their own tale.

There's tart and nutty.
There's bitter and spicy.
There's savory and minty.
There's sour and dicey.

My father is a painter,
but he doesn't use a brush.
This meal is a masterpiece
I wouldn't dare rush.

Sushi is made with raw fish.
That means, it's fish that
hasn't been cooked.

But I think it might be *too* raw
because everywhere I looked,
it looked.

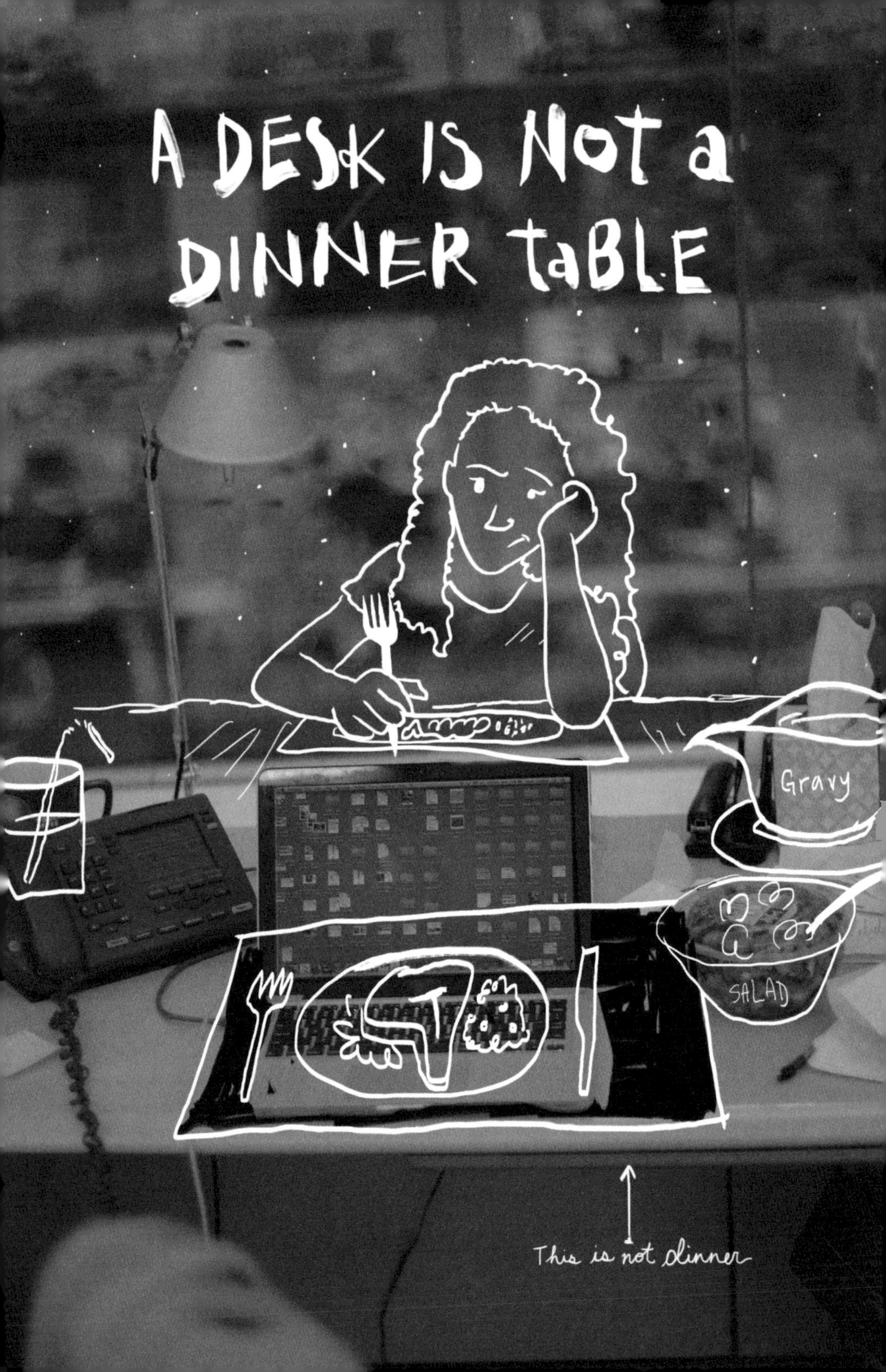
A DESK IS NOT A DINNER TABLE
Gravy
SALAD
This is not dinner

You can eat dinner
at a round table
or a square table.
An oblong table
or a pear-shaped table.

But a desk
is not a dinner table.

You can eat dinner at the beach
or eat it on a boat.
Eat it in a bikini
or eat it in a coat.
Eat it upstairs.
Eat it outside.
Eat it feeling fat
or feeling thinner.

But a desk? No.
A desk is not a place for dinner.

Call it "food in face."
Call it "stuffing belly."
Call it the Internet
with toast and jelly.

Dinner at a desk
needs a re-label.
Because a desk
will never be a dinner table.

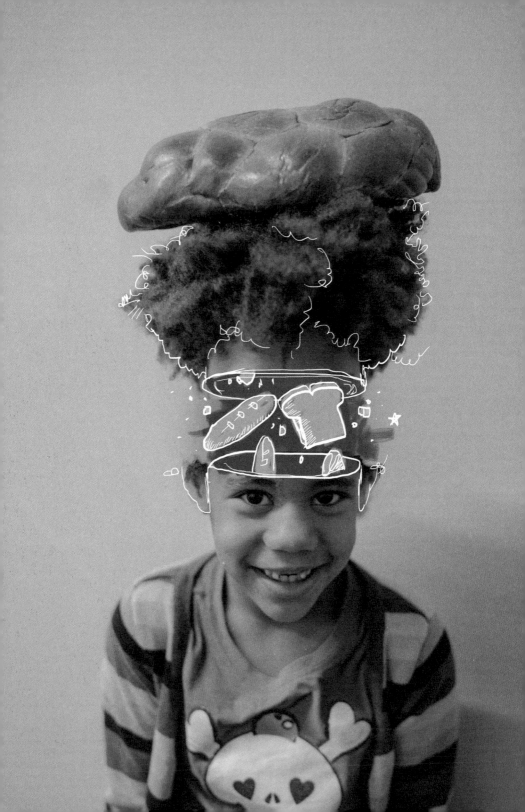

BREAD DREAMS

Everyone seems concerned about
the bread I wear upon my head.
This is not such a crazy thing,
after all my favorite food is bread.
And when I want to sleep
I take a loaf to pillow me.
And I dream
I dream
I dream

of pumpernickel and baguettes,
of sourdough and rye,
crumpets and crêpes,
some buttery, some dry.

Chapati and roti,
naan and wheat,
sometimes salty,
sometimes sweet.

But if I eat too much bread,
I'll fall asleep
sleep
sleep.

Sleep.

Old George Washington Carver

(didn't invent peanut butter)

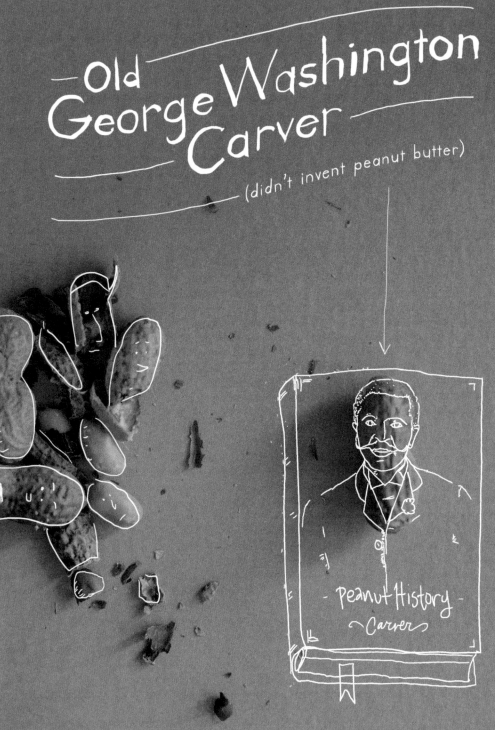

Peanut History
~Carver~

Old George Washington Carver
did not invent peanut butter.

He invented lamp oil and shaving cream,
laundry soap and shampoo,
peanut flour, leather dye,
all this from a peanut or two.

But old George Washington Carver
did not invent peanut butter.

He made soap to clean your hands
and diesel fuel for your cars.
He made ink to print on signs,
all from the same nuts inside your jars.

But old George Washington Carver
did not invent peanut butter.

Some scientists use beakers
with chemicals and such,
but old George Washington Carver
stuck to peanuts and sweet-potato guts.

I hate to break it to you,
the truth is tough to utter.
But old George Washington Carver
did not invent peanut butter.

CORN

Existential Crisis
Which came first, the corn or the cob?
(Or the butter?)

The Jig Is Up
Corn says to the cob,
"I think I'm going to get canned."

Identity Crisis
Corn says to the cob,
"Are we white or yellow?"
Cob says back,
"I don't see color, I just see kernels."

Nostalgia
Cob says to the corn,
"Remember when we were just young stalks in the field?"

Mutton used to be sheep.
Beef used to be cows.
Seafood used to swim the sea.
Pigs are pork now.
An animal gets a new name
when it becomes a new meal.
But what was the animal
that we call veal?

Runaway Beans

Toot!

Excuse me, Miss, have you seen my beans?

I think I lost them in the subway.

Peep!

I used to hate the little things,

'til I learned they gave me energy.

Poot!

They make me toot and poot and beep.

I toot so hard, I fly out of my seat.

Bonk!

Pardon me, Miss, I really need some help.

My beans wouldn't just run away by themselves.

Wonk!

So if you hear a toot or peep! or poot!

Or bonk or wonk or wap

or pop or crackle or zap

or snap or fap or zing,

will you please, oh please

give me a ring?

I think I lost them in the subway.

BOOSTER

There's something special about this chicken dinner,
but the reason, I can't quite finger.
It's soft and kind and supple and sweet
and makes me happy down to my feet.

It's so juicy and delectable, and my mouth's a perfect fit.
I think it smells like heaven, but that's not it.
There's something familiar about this chicken dinner,
but what, I still have yet to figure.

With every bite I take, I want to cock-a-doodle-doo.
But wait. Is that an empty chicken coop?
There's something special about this chicken dinner,
and the reason is, I think I just ate my pet rooster, Booster.

(And he tastes so good.)

I AM a FARMER

I am a farmer but I don't
    have a farm.
Just a tiny little garden in
    my front yard.
I am a farmer, and if I had my way,
I'd have a chicken-coop mailbox
    with eggs and hay.

I'd trade my dog for a goat.
I'd trade my cat for a cow.
I'd plant veggies in my gutters,
but I'd skip the plow.

I'd have my chickens
    in that mailbox coop,
and a farmer's market on my stoop.
I'd play my boom box
    to add some charm
but no country music,
    'cause this is still not a farm.

GOATS

Ashley Won't Eat It If She Can't Spell It

"Ashley won't eat it if she can't spell it," Ashley said.
(She spoke in third person,
a habit she picked up from all the books she's read.)

When she went to the store,
her mother would read the package ingredients.

"Ashley won't eat it if she can't spell it," Ashley said.

Her mother thought it was a safe bet
when she reached for the bread.

    "Let's see, there's flour?"
"F .. L .. O .. U .. R, check!"
    "Salt?"
"S .. A .. L .. T, check!"
    "Yeast?"
"Y .. E .. A .. S .. T, check!"
    "Oil?"
"O .. I .. L, cha-check!"
    "Azo-di-car-bona-mide?"
"A .. Z .. O .. D ... I guess there will be no bread for me.
I mean, no bread for Ashley," Ashley said.

"'Cause Ashley won't eat it if she can't spell it."

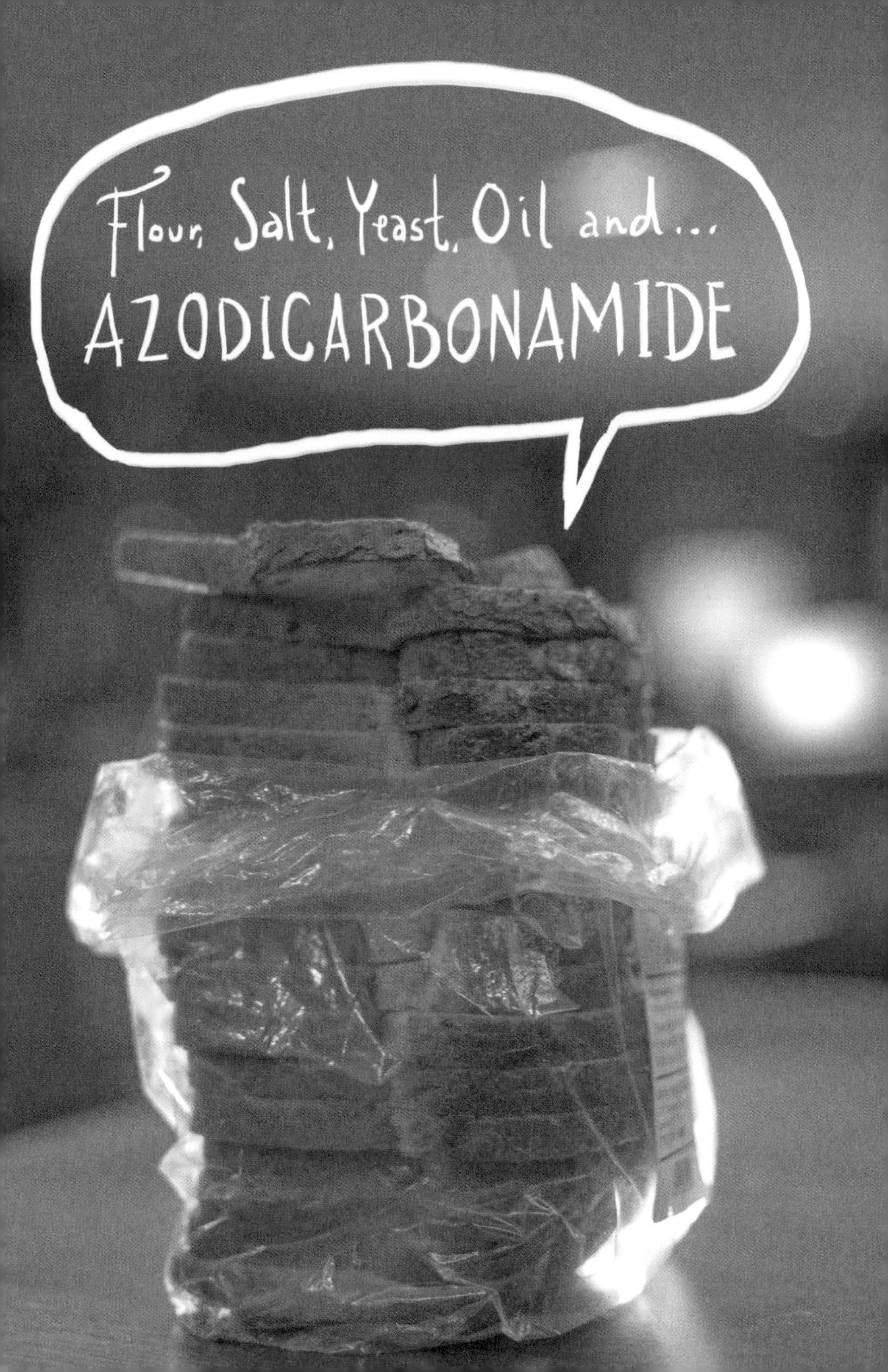
Flour, Salt, Yeast, Oil and...
AZODICARBONAMIDE

SLIPPERY NOODLES

Twirl them, whirl them,
slop them, slip them,
twist them, curl them,
whip them, flip them,
sip them, slurp them,
chew them, beat them.
But you must use a fork
when you eat them.

Slurp it up, mash it up,
cut it up, clap it up,
look it up, pass it up,
turn it up, flap it up,
shake it up, make it up,
smell it up, love it up.
But do not use your hands
when you eat it up.

This is an odd diet food.
The box said, "Lose weight in a day!"
But this can't be good,
because my whole body just went away.

DEAR MICHELLE OBAMA,

Can you teach me
how to garden like you?
I've seen all your gardening
videos on YouTube.
Your cabbage sure
does look purple,
and your blueberries
are brighter than the moon.

Can you teach me how
to garden so pretty?
'Cause we got a tiny apartment
in Long Island City.
I got no field, like you.
I got no hills.
But I got two
little windowsills.

I got no landscapers.
I got no help
except my little brother,
and he's no help.
I got no tools
like gloves or spades
except these digging spoons
that I made.

I saw your garden Twitter pics.
Your hair was so pretty.
So when I start planting,
my barrettes will be with me.
My first plant is
gonna be tomatoes,
'cause my momma said
my clay pots can grow those.

But, I think she said that
'cause I'm just a kid. Pshh.
What's the first thing
that *you* planted?

'Cause someday my garden
is gonna look like yours,
with carrots and apples
and grapes in scores.

All of Long Island City
is gonna buy my food too.
If you can teach me how
to garden like you.

Truly yours,

AMAYA

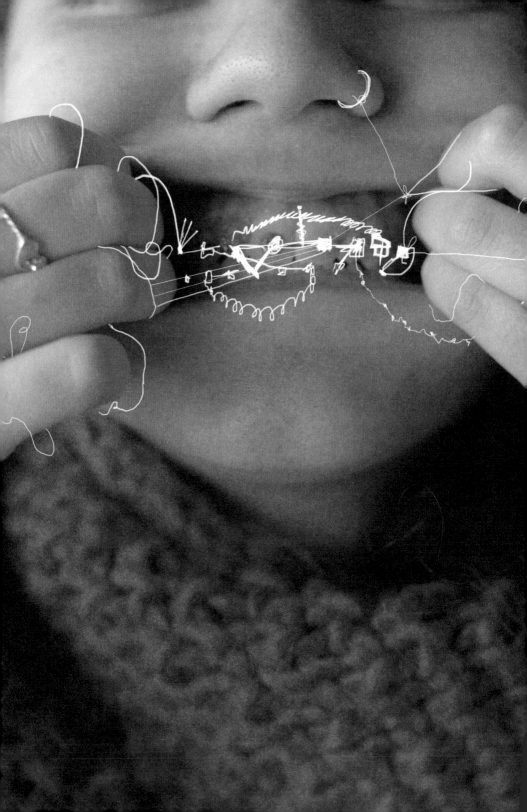

HUNGRY

My face is full of braces.
My plate is full of meat.
And all the things I love so much
but don't know how to eat.

The Saddest Happiest Meal

"Oh, how did I get like this?" wailed the burger.
"For once I was a cow that grazed the fields of Yonder."

"Oh, how did we get like this?" wailed the fries.
"For once we were a tater with little spots for eyes."

"Oh, how did I get like this?" wailed the drink.
"For once I was...wait...who was I? Oh, just sugar, I think."

Red Rooster, Red Rooster

Red Rooster, Red Rooster,
you truly are a gem.
I'm not talking about a singing bird.
I'm talking, the restaurant in Harlem.

When we came by Sunday morning,
we could not find an empty chair.
You were packed with all these sweet old ladies
with big red hats upon their hair.

We came back that afternoon,
we could not get a seat.
You had a jazz band playing.
They were swinging to the beat.

We came back Sunday night,
this time with a reservation.
We sat at our cushy booth,
no time for conversation.

Before the waiter even gave me a menu,
I ordered faster than the breeze.
I pointed to the picture on the wall.
"I'll have the red rooster, please."

The waiter was surprised. "I'm sorry but
we don't actually serve red roosters, I fear."
"Well, if all these people aren't eating red roosters,"
I said, "What are they doing here?"

Red Rooster, Red Rooster,
you truly are a gem.
You got all these people fooled,
thinking they can eat a red rooster in Harlem.

Would You Eat Green Eggs With Dye?

I would not like green eggs with dye.
I would not like my bread bleached white.

I would not like my drink turned blue.
I would not like my greens cooked brown.
I would not like my muffins teal
Please, don't change the colors of my meal.

DOCTOR FOOD

There's something funny about Doctor Food.
He doesn't seem like a doctor to me.
He never prescribes medicine,
but he always prescribes a recipe.

I called him once when I wanted to gag.
I had something bad for dinner.
The doctor said, "No problem!
Just make some tea with ginger."

One day I had a case of the *sad faces*,
my frown was stiff as a tree.
He said a salmon fillet will do the trick,
they're chock-full of vitamin D.

And when I was tired day after day,
my head as heavy as a moose,
he said, "You can put pep in your step,
just drink a big glass of orange juice."

But when I told the doctor I broke my arm,
jumping out of a willow tree,
the doctor said, "I've got nothing for that.
There's no cure for stupidity."

Hot Soup

She wanted to try the soup,
but the soup was just too hot.
She blew and blew and whistled and huffed,
but she could not cool the pot.

She decided to sip it anyway.
She could not, would not wait!
But when she burned her tiny tongue,
it (sort of) set her straight.

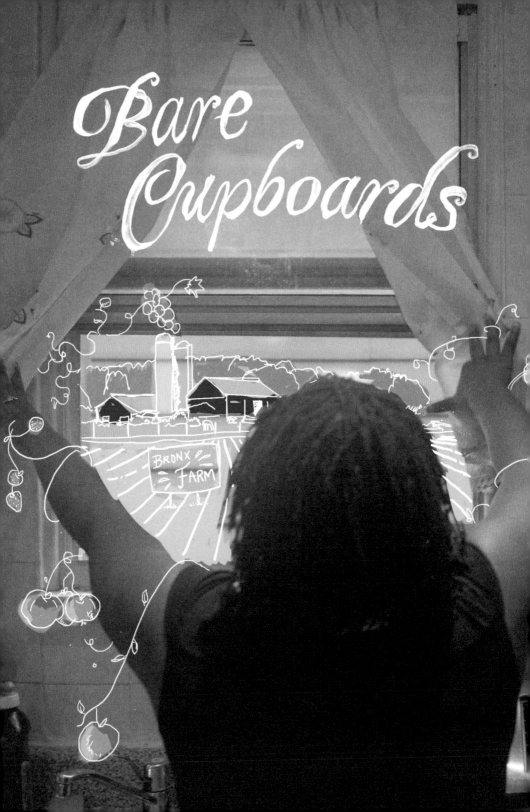

I don't know where
our next meal will come from.
The fridge is empty
and the cupboards are dry.
I wonder if we can
grow some food outside.

LUCK

If I had my own COOKING SHOW

If I had my own cooking show,
oh, the things I'd make...
spider noodles with ant balls
and baked mud cakes.

If I had my own cooking show,
I'd wave to all the girls I know.
I'd make them caramel-covered frogs
and wrap them up with pretty bows.

If I had my own cooking show,
I'd call it "The Dilly-Dallyin' Cooking Show"
and I'd teach the most Dilly-Dallyin' recipes I know.
'Cause it's my own cooking show.

Selfish Shelbi

Shelbi was the kind of girl who didn't like to share.

So when she heard bacteria helped her tummy eat she said it was unfair.

PET Cabbage

I lost my pet cabbage, but how is that?
I dressed it with a feather upon its hat.
It used to be round and purple and plump,
but then it got squishy and smelled like a dump.

I left it alone with my mom one day.
She said it ran off when she looked away.
But I don't think that could be true
'cause that's just not something my cabbage would do.

Pet dog

Pet cabbage ♡

Gramma's Magic Recipes

Gramma has magic Jamaican recipes
but they're not in any book.
I can't find them anywhere
no matter where I look.

Her oxtail stew makes you
jump and kick.
Her curry chicken?
It vanishes quick.

Her ackee and saltfish
sharpens your wit.
And the goat-head soup
will make you flip.

I swear, I've seen
her porridge heal the sick.
She knows a thing or two
about tasty tricks.

Gramma has magic Jamaican recipes.
I wish she'd write them down.
'Cause when my *dad* makes oxtail stew,
it's not magic, it's just brown.

LAB-COAT CORN

It looks like corn
It feels like corn
It smells like corn
It even tastes like corn.
You can butter it like corn
You can bake it in a pot pie
You can fry it 'til it pops
or add it to stir fry.

But even if it looks like corn
and it feels like corn,
if the corn is born in a lab
instead of on crop land,
and raised by lab coats
instead of farm hands,
is it corn at all?

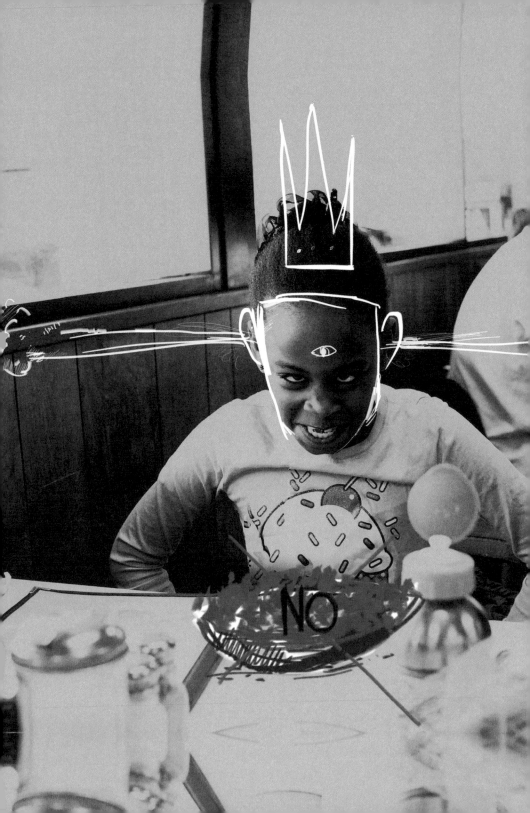

NO MORE BEETS

I'd sooner lick the cat
than eat more beets.
I'd sooner kiss the dog
than eat more beets.
I'd rake the lawn
and clean the gutters
for our whole street.
I'd sooner do anything
than eat more beets.

The Indifferent Plate

Nothing matters to the plate,
no, nothing matters really.
You can fill it with delicious steak
or the worst-tasting chili.

There could be no more food on earth.
The world could meet doomsday.
You could get skinny or fat,
but the plate would never say.

'Cause nothing matters to the plate.

DINNER PARTY

We bought a table.
We bought some chairs.
We bought some placemats
and silverware.

We bought candles,
and a centerpiece with flowers.
We set down plates
and it took us hours.

We've got cooks.
We've got guests.
We've got ice
inside a chest.

We've got glasses in pairs.
We've said our prayers.

Mom and Dad are kissing.
But there's still something missing.

Everybody's in the eating mood.
Wait.
Where's the food?

Vegetables don't grow in cans.

Bread doesn't grow in bags.

Juice doesn't grow in cartons.

Potatoes don't grow in sacks.

Chickens don't grow shrink-wrapped.

Steaks don't grow on Styrofoam.

Fruit doesn't grow in cups.

Butter doesn't grow in paper.

Cheese doesn't grow in wax.

Cucumbers don't grow in jars.

Because food doesn't grow in packages.

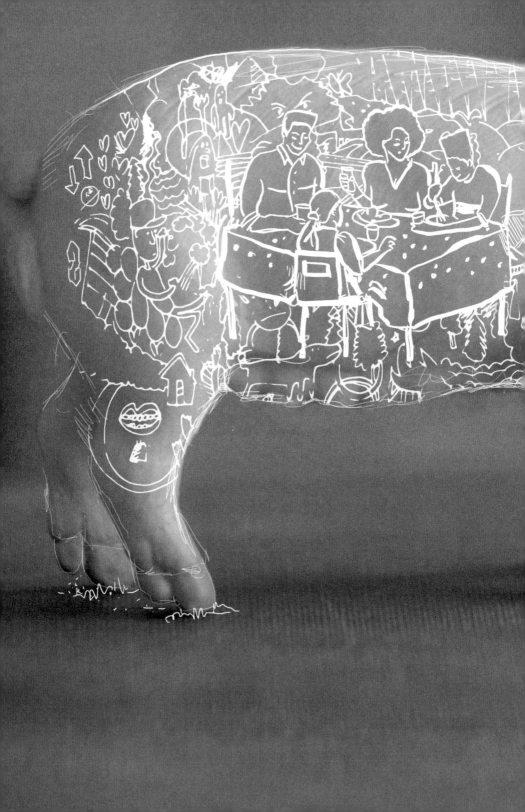

Family Chitterlings

Mommy eats chitterlings.
Daddy eats chitterlings.
Uncle Walter, Uncle Glen eat chitterlings.
Aunt Phyllis, Aunt Diane eat chitterlings.
Cousin Greta loves chitterlings.
Even sister Crystal eats chitterlings.

They all think I'm funny for not eating them too.
But every time, I say, "The joke's on you."
'Cause they don't know chitterlings are pig guts.
And that's why they smell like pig poo.

STOP TOUCHING MY FOOD

When I tried to serve him casserole,
Grampa said, "Who's been touching this food?
Farmers, packers and shippers,
coolers for summer and heaters for winter,
processors, pickers, inspectors,
pokers, traps and injectors.
The truck guy, the store guy,
the bagger, then you?
Too many people touching my food.
Stop touching my food.

Your grandmother used to pick vegetables
from our garden in the back,
and I'd cook them on the stove
and that was that.

I think it's terribly rude...
all these people touching my food.
So, stop touching my food."

Maybe Grampa just doesn't like casserole.

DO IT for Dr. KING

Please, please eat those greens.
Dr. King's Dream was a big dream.
When I say a big dream, I mean a green dream.
He dreamed, that you'd eat those greens.
He dreamed, we'd love all the colors at our table:
brown, pink, black, white and especially your greens.
You have got to eat your greens.
So sit in that chair and eat them, before I get mean
and eat those greens for Dr. King.

A GREEN DREAM

Do it for Dr. King

Okay, I confess the green dream is my dream.

But you still have to eat your greens!

Love
Eshabazz

I Didn't Steal Your Mangos

There's a mango thief on the loose!
He was carrying a sack.
I was walking down the street
when I caught him in the act.

I said, "You're caught, Mango Thief!
Unhand those mangos now!"
He threw that big sack down
and ran off like a mad cow.

I only took a few,
the ones I'm eating now.
You asked how I got your mangos,
well, now you know how.

It wasn't me.
I didn't steal your mangos.

There's a small food desert in Harlem
where you can't find fresh foods.
But they never talk about this,
when I watch the news.

If you think you've seen a fruit stand,
it's only a mirage.
It's a painting of a pineapple
on the side of a garage.

There's a small food desert in Harlem,
and it's a big shame,
'cause there are so many stores
full of junk food and brand names.

You see, broccoli has no logo.
There's no sales rep for fresh kale.
So if you want green beans and sweet potatoes,
you have to eat the canned food on sale.

If you're in that small food desert in Harlem.

LONG BONE

This chicken bone is long,
longer than I can eat.
It would help if I bit it slow,
and only ate the meat.

SOMETIMES...

Chicken tastes sooo good, you may think that they are magical. BUT, don't be fooled, there is nothing magical about chickens. UNICORNS, on the other hand, are always magical but don't always taste sooo good.

Supper was great, and Ruby Loo ate,
and I mean *ate*...

Turkey, cranberry, greens, rice,
biscuits with gravy, tea with ice,
peas and ham and her favorite...carrot cake.
Who can eat all that goodness, for goodness sake?

Ruby Loo could, or at least she'd try.
Somehow her stomach was smaller than her eyes.
Yes. Her stomach was smaller than her eyes.
Oh, no. Her stomach was smaller than her eyes.

She ate and ate and ate and ate,
until her tummy started to roar.
"Run!" it roared. "Ruuuun!"
So she ran to the bathroom and slammed the door.

"I ate and ate and ate and ate,
I ate too much goodness, for goodness sake,
and now my belly roars with ache,
before I got my carrot cake."

She didn't cry, but she felt sort of duped.
And that's why Ruby Loo drooped when she pooped.

Chaz and the $100 APPLE

"What could make an apple cost one hundred bucks?
Will it gush like a river?
Will it have gold inside?
Will it make me time travel to another time?
Will it do a dance? Will it sing a song?
Will it put a suit on and go to the prom?"

"No!" yelled Chaz, the fruit market man,
holding the apple tenderly in his hands.

"Oookaayy," I said. "So I'd still like to know,
what can make an apple worth one hundred bucks?"

His nose turned up and then he replied,
"Because I said so, isn't that enough?
Would you ask a mother the worth of her child?
Perhaps something cheap will suffice.
How much does it cost for love itself?
Apples are priceless.
I know you didn't mean to offend,
but, you see, this very last apple is my very last friend.
That's what makes an apple cost one hundred bucks."

An apple a day keeps the Heartache away.

Mr. Pace said the Longest Grace

Mr. Pace said the longest grace.

Just as everyone was ready to eat, and all the seniors
put in their teeth, Mr. Pace said the longest grace.

At Thanksgiving dinner, we unfolded our napkins, and
poured gravy on our stuffing. Just as we had knives and
forks in hand, Mr. Pace said the longest grace.

> "Thank you for this day.
> Thank you for these friends.
> Thank you for this food...
> Wait, let me start again."

And again. And again. Will he ever say Amen?

Mr. Pace said the longest grace.

When a rattlesnake up and bit him, and he was dying
from the venom in him, the doctor sent an emergency note...
a snake-bite kit with antidote. If only he had read the note and
swallowed up the antidote. That's all, you see, he really needed,
but he bowed his head and thus proceeded...

> "Thank you for this day.
> Thank you for these friends
> Thank you for this..."

Mr. Pace said his shortest grace.

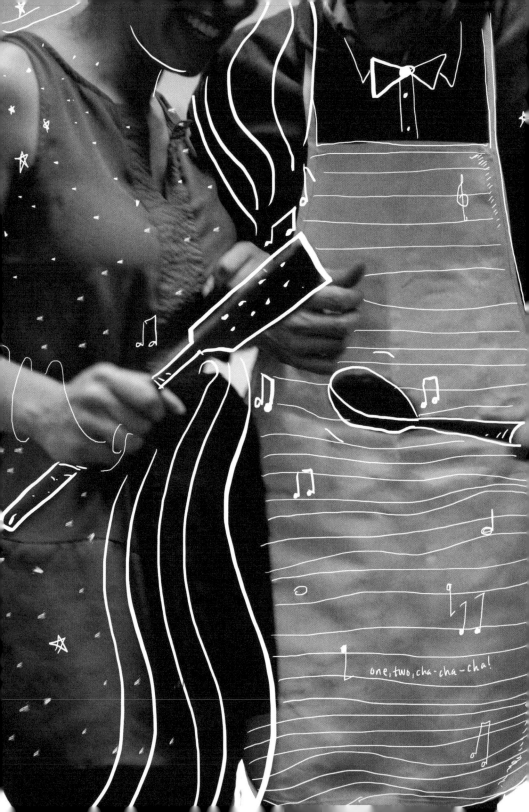

DANCING
KITCHEN

You're flipping, mixing and dancing too.
You're baking, sautéing and sizzling food.

Steam a potato,
add a spice.
Splash olive oil
in yellow rice.
Cook something different.
Same is old news.
Turn up the music...
Wear your dancing shoes.

You're flipping, mixing and dancing too.
You're baking, sautéing and sizzling food.

And now we're cooking, in a dancing kitchen!

You're baking, sautéing and sizzling food.
So, keep flipping, mixing and dancing too.

The Last Pea

If I eat one more pea,
I think I will explode.
I'm telling you.
If I
eat
one
more
pea
I will certainly explode...

Who am I kidding.
I only have one pea left.
I might as well...

Author's Note

I think that learning to cook for yourself is a requirement for being a grownup.

The best meal I've ever eaten was one that I imagined in a day dream on a hungry day.

I have the peculiar habit of writing poems and bringing them to parties as gifts — that's how this book was born.

I wrote this book to inspire people to read poems at dinner time.

For best taste, read these poems just before dinner.

EAT GREEN. I always dance in the kitchen. I can't tell the difference between A KITCHEN FLOOR AND a DANCE FLOOR.

My father used to cook me something called "CHI GETTI!" To this day, I still have no idea what was in it.

My gramma is Jamaican and really knows magic. Sometimes she teaches me tricks.

I have never eaten a pet of mine, but I love purple cabbage.

Much of my graffiti is inspired by Jean-Michel Basquiat. He liked to write smart words instead of just his name.

DINNER TIME IS THE BEST TIME ♡

My wife's name is Ashley but she eats things she can't spell sometimes. She's with me in that picture to the right →

♡X

My wife's family loves chitterlings — but not me!

My mother makes the world's best fried chicken and has cooked me more meals than anyone else in the world.

My favorite food is anything Jamaican.

Upon finishing this book, I found out I might have to eat gluten-free! Can someone tell me what gluten is?

MY GRANDMOTHER used to have a garden in the back yard and pick the vegetables right before she cooked them. It still amazes me that you can put seeds in the ground and a few days later food will come out. I have my own garden.

A family that eats together speaks together

with love Eric-Shabazz Larkin